# FIVE-MINUTE WARM-UPS

## FOR THE MIDDLE GRADES

## REVISED EDITION

Quick-and-Easy Activities
To Reinforce Basic Skills

by Bea Green, Sandi Schlichting, and Mary Ellen Thomas

Incentive Publications, Inc.
Nashville, Tennessee

Special acknowledgement
is accorded to Marjorie Frank
for compiling and organizing
the materials included in this revision.

*Cover by Kristy Jones*
*Edited by Charlotte Bosarge*
ISBN 0-86530-626-5

2    3    4    5    6    7    8    9    10         07     06     05     04

PRINTED IN THE UNITED STATES OF AMERICA
www.incentivepublications.com

# Table of Contents

# SOCIAL STUDIES

# SCIENCE

# BONUS: SELF-AWARENESS ACTIVITIES

# INTRODUCTION

Think about all those times during the school day or school week when there are just five or ten minutes remaining before the class must move on to something else. These are time periods of an unusual length—too short to start a major event or lesson but too long to waste. Such a spell of a time may be just before lunch, just before recess, while you're waiting to send the class to P.E. or music, or while you're waiting for a class visitor. Maybe there are a few minutes at the start of the class when you aren't quite ready to dive into a long lesson, or at the end of the class when you've put everything away and don't want to waste valuable time.

Even with the best planning, it is not possible to eliminate those extra five-minute periods. However, when you do a little calculation, you'll realize that five minutes a day adds up to over fifteen hours during a school year—almost two full days of valuable instructional time! Those odd extra moments can be put to excellent use with little or no preparation at all. *Five-Minute Warm-ups for the Middle Grades* provides just what you need to use these small pockets of time for effective reinforcement of skills and concepts in language, math, science, and social studies.

These warm-ups are more than just ways to fill extra moments. You will find that they spark enthusiasm in students, "warm them up" for the next activity, or leave them "fired-up" with learning as they exit the class. Many of these warm-ups can be used as lead-ins for a new unit or lesson. Others are meant for sharpening basic skills and facts. Some are simply fun-filled ways to put skills and knowledge to work, but just about all of them can be extended into much longer learning lessons.

The book ends with a bonus section of self-awareness activities. The wise middle grades teacher knows when the atmosphere of trust in a classroom has reached a level where such activities can be of benefit to the group. At first, students may seem reluctant to participate in self-awareness activities. However, when you present them in a non-coercive way and repeat them regularly, you will probably find that these are the activities students most want to extend beyond the five-minute time period.

Now that you have this treasure of short, useful activities with high student appeal, you need not dread those extra moments in your school day's schedule. Indeed, you will look forward to the lulls when you can delight the students with quick but important warm-ups!

Happy Teaching!

# Language Arts

Language Arts

*Language Arts*

Language Arts

**Language Arts**

Language Arts

*Language Arts*

Language Arts

**Language Arts**

# SPECTACULAR STARTS

Challenge students to improve their writing by polishing the skill of good beginnings. Show them an "ordinary" beginning and a "spectacular" beginning. (See example below.) Then, give them a writing topic. Let them brainstorm spectacular opening sentences for that topic. Encourage them to think of starters that will grab the reader's attention and compel him or her to keep on reading. Enlist one student to record the ideas.

Ordinary:        On Friday, our class took the long-anticipated trip to the aquarium.

Spectacular:   No one in our class could ever have imagined how Friday's trip to the aquarium would turn out.

OR

I don't know who was more amazed by Friday's trip to the aquarium— our class, or the sharks.

# ARGUMENTS IN A HURRY

Tell the students to imagine that they have a younger sister (or brother, or neighbor) who is on her (or his) way to get a large tattoo. They only have five minutes to convince the sister not to do this. Position one student at the chalkboard so he is ready to write the arguments down as they are offered.

Try these *Arguments in a Hurry* on other days:
- ✦ **Persuade your school to let you bring pets to class.**
- ✦ **Convince your parents to get you a motorcycle.**
- ✦ **Argue that kids should not be allowed to use the Internet.**
- ✦ **Persuade a friend to take care of your pet boa constrictor for a week.**
- ✦ **Argue that the voting age should be lowered to 12.**
- ✦ **Persuade your school staff to try a "no homework" policy.**

# QUICK COLLECTIONS

Brainstorm all the words you can gather in five minutes that fit into one of these categories. Get a student (or the teacher) to keep a written list of the words.

| | | |
|---|---|---|
| slow words | night words | city words |
| fast words | day words | country words |
| small words | color words | laughing words |
| big words | tasty words | creepy words |
| lazy words | salty words | sickly words |
| energetic words | dry words | grumpy words |
| cool words | wet words | mysterious words |
| hot words | confusing words | heavy words |
| troublesome words | long-distance words | light words |

Save the word collections. Use them another day to write short stories, paragraphs, poems, or descriptions.

# PARAGRAPH DETECTIVES

Write this paragraph on the board ahead of time. Tell students to read it quickly.

A noise this terrible had never been heard in a library. At least, Charles and Delilah could not imagine that it had. The noise was shocking, ugly, pained, and horrifying. It came from somewhere in the biography section, they were sure. Was it a cry for help? Was there someone hiding or hurt between the bookshelves? After they heard the noise the fourth time, Charles cautiously went to investigate, creeping slowly down the aisle between the stacks of books. Again, the horrendous moan burst forth, right ahead of him. He saw no one. The moan came another time, louder still. As it did, a book fell to the floor at his feet. The pages were violently torn from the binding. Charles touched the book gently, and heard a low sigh, "Ahhhhh." He read the title: *Trapped Between the Covers.* The author was Sandra Paige.

Ask students to do some paragraph detecting to quickly answer questions such as these:

✦ **How many times was a noise made? (6—shocking noise 5 times, sigh 1 time)**

✦ **How many people heard the shocking noise? (2, for sure)**

✦ **What words describe the noise? (terrible, shocking, ugly, pained, terrifying)**

✦ **How did Charles approach the book? (cautiously, gently)**

✦ **Under what letter was the book shelved? (P for the author's name—it is a biography.)**

# WHO OWNS THE CAMEL?

Give students a copy of the following logic problem. Tell them they will need to use logical reasoning skills to solve the problem. Suggest that they create a diagram or chart to help them think through the problem. Challenge them to find the answer in only five minutes.

Four neighbors live in four houses in a row. Each house is a different color. Each inhabitant has a different pet and a different hobby. Use the clues below to answer the question, *"Who owns the camel?"*

1. The owner of the white house has a pet tarantula.
2. Charlie lives between George and Zelda.
3. The scuba diver lives in the first house on the left.
4. Margaret has a pet boa constrictor.
5. The owner of the red house is a hula dancer.
6. The blue house is next to the green house.
7. The scuba diver lives next to the red house.
8. The skunk lives next door to the pet tarantula.
9. The skydiver lives next door to the hula dancer.
10. Zelda lives in the blue house.
11. The white house is not next to the green house.
12. The ventriloquist's pet is not a mammal.
13. Charlie is terrified of spiders.
14. Neither George nor Zelda lives in the green house.

(Answer: *Zelda*)

---

# A BUBBLEGUM BROTHER

It's great fun to compare people to food. Such an exercise sharpens creative thinking and expands the use of figurative language. Give the students one or more examples of similes that compare a person to a food (extended to explain the comparison). Then ask each student to write or say a simile comparing a person and a food.

Examples:
- **My little brother is like bubblegum because he sticks to me everywhere I go.**
- **Sally is like an apple because everything she does is so healthy.**
- **Grandma is warm and comfortable like a macaroni-cheese casserole.**
- **Lucy is as sour as a dill pickle. She is always complaining!**

Try comparing people to animals, toys, vehicles, or other things that will stretch the imagination and produce creative similes.

# CLEVER CONTRADICTIONS

Explain to students what an oxymoron is. Then gather as many as they can think of in five minutes. You might challenge them to be on the lookout for more oxymorons, and work to build an ongoing compilation of them. Oxymorons are fun and challenging. Students will build vocabulary and critical thinking skills as they collect oxymorons.

Examples:

| | | | |
|---|---|---|---|
| jumbo shrimp | act natural | true counterfeit | found missing |
| civil war | slow speed | down escalator | near miss |
| walking dead | awfully good | sweet tarts | grounded flight |
| fresh frozen | old news | good grief | |
| larger half | pretty awful | virtual reality | |

# WHAT'S WRONG?

Send students on a "scavenger hunt" for punctuation and capitalization errors. Give each student a half-sheet of notebook paper. Ask them to write 2-3 sentences that contain deliberate errors in punctuation and capitalization. Encourage them to include a variety of proper nouns and adjectives that should be capitalized, and to capitalize some things that should not be capitalized. Set a timer for 2 minutes.

When the timer rings, trade papers. Use the last 3 minutes to track down the errors and fix them. Each student will be challenged to find the errors in sentences written by another student.

Example:

> shortly after valentine;s Day, on February 23 2004 we visited these places; the golden gate Bridge, orlando florida and the rocky mountains. what fun we had riding Roller Coasters, swimming in the gulf of Mexico and climbing Peaks? Let's do this every year "we said to our parents".

# OBJECT SWITCH

Review with students the description of direct objects and indirect objects:

*Georgia brought her friends to the ballgame.* (Friends is a direct object.)
*Georgia gave her friends free tickets.* (Friends is the indirect object.)

Ask students to show their understanding of direct and indirect objects by changing one into the other!

Start with a word used as a direct object. Ask them to use it as an indirect object.

Then use a word as an indirect object. Ask them to find it and write a sentence where it is used as a direct object.

Examples:      Cat is a direct object: *Tom scared the cat.*
Switch "cat" to indirect object: *Tom gave the cat a hug.*

Ball is the indirect object: *Charlene gave the ball a whack.*
Switch "ball" to direct object: *Charlene hit the ball.*

# MULTIPLE IDENTITIES

Some words can be nouns as well as adjectives or verbs—they have "multiple identities." Solidify grammar skills by tracking down words that can be used in different ways. Group students in pairs. Give each pair one of the following words. Ask them to write at least two sentences, each using the word as a different part of speech. (In some cases, the words can be used as more than two different parts of speech.) If time permits, ask students to think of other words with "multiple identities."

Examples:

| | | | | |
|---|---|---|---|---|
| **run** | **melted** | **awakening** | **fly** | **rose** |
| **out** | **rush** | **launch** | **solid** | **harness** |
| **green** | **dance** | **hand** | **shouting** | **frightening** |
| **answer** | **light** | **spotted** | **horse** | **star** |
| **drop** | **firm** | **cheers** | **broken** | |

# CLEAR THE CONFUSION

Some sentences just don't make sense. Or, they seem to give a message that is not what the writer intended. Divide the students into small groups (3-4 students). Give an unclear sentence to each group. Give them two minutes to rewrite the sentence so it makes sense. Let each group share the confusing sentence and the clarified sentence.

- ✦ **Simone enjoyed her ham sandwich listening to the radio.**
- ✦ **Elizabeth discussed names for her new cat talking to her friend on the cell phone.**
- ✦ **We were harassed by a shark sailing our boat.**
- ✦ **Chewing on a shoe, Julie caught her puppy.**
- ✦ **We saw the escaped elephant watching television.**
- ✦ **She and Tom met them and they climbed into their car.**
- ✦ **The principal noticed dogs on the playground outside his window talking on the telephone.**
- ✦ **Max was distracted by the noisy neighbors doing his homework.**
- ✦ **Sam caught a marlin fishing from the yacht.**

# USAGE MIX-UPS

See how fast your students can clear up all these mix-ups in language usage.

*(Corrected version)*

| | |
|---|---|
| ✦ **Scarcely nobody visits this place.** | **(Scarcely anybody visits this place.)** |
| ✦ **Do not feed nothing to the hippo.** | **(Do not feed anything to the hippo.)** |
| ✦ **Abby she got a new tattoo yesterday.** | **(Abby got a new tattoo yesterday.)** |
| ✦ **No screaming is never allowed here.** | **(No screaming is ever allowed here.)** |
| ✦ **You would of screamed, too.** | **(You would have screamed, too.)** |
| ✦ **This here is a man-eating fish.** | **(This is a man-eating fish.)** |
| ✦ **Where is the lifeguard at?** | **(Where is the lifeguard?)** |
| ✦ **Remember to not swim alone.** | **(Remember not to swim alone.)** |
| ✦ **I can't see monsters anywheres!** | **(I can't see monsters anywhere.)** |
| ✦ **Don't sit your lunch near the zebra.** | **(Don't set your lunch near the zebra.)** |
| ✦ **The tiger just rose up her head.** | **(The tiger just raised up her head.)** |
| ✦ **Is that a snake laying in the mud?** | **(Is that a snake lying in the mud?)** |
| ✦ **Will those there lobsters bite me?** | **(Will those lobsters bite me?)** |

# THAT'S A DIRECT QUOTE!

Writing quotations properly can be tricky! Here's a quick way to give students practice in writing and punctuating direct quotations correctly. Ask them to change sentences about someone saying something into direct quotes. Read a sentence such as one of those below. Let pairs or groups take turns changing the sentence so that it includes a quotation.

Examples:

✦ **Zeke's friend promised to buy him a pizza.**
   **With a quotation: Zeke's friend promised, "I'll buy you a pizza."**
✦ **The teacher told me I had been tardy too many times.**
   **With a quotation: "You've been tardy too many times," the teacher told me.**
✦ **Who is screaming that the house is on fire?**
   **With a quotation: Who is screaming, "The house is on fire!"**
✦ **Roxie asked Sam if he was going to the rock concert.**
   **With a quotation: "Are you going to the rock concert, Sam?" asked Roxie.**

---

# SIMILAR WORDS

Each sentence below has a wrong word that interferes with the meaning of the sentence. The word sounds and looks similar to the correct word, but it is not quite right! Write sentences such as these on the chalkboard, or give students copies. Have them track down the troublesome word and replace it with the correct word.

Examples:

✦ **That ice cream shop doesn't except checks.**          (except—accept)
✦ **You have a bad altitude about your math class.**          (altitude—attitude)
✦ **I just drank a whole cartoon of chocolate milk.**          (cartoon—carton)
✦ **I was lucky to allude that alligator that was chasing me.**          (allude—elude)
✦ **You were lucky to meet that imminent politician.**          (imminent—eminent)
✦ **My sister keeps her secret dairy hidden in her closet.**          (dairy—diary)
✦ **The burglar insured me that he would not shoot anybody.**          (insured—assured)
✦ **I wonder witch one has the poison ivy?**          (witch—which)
✦ **Jody asked her boss for a raise in her celery today.**          (celery—salary)

# BEGINNINGS AND ENDINGS

To practice using prefixes and suffixes, give students one of the examples below. Ask them to name words containing that prefix or suffix. When they run out of examples, go to another.

| Prefixes: | uni- | dis- | mis- | im- | maxi- | super- |
|---|---|---|---|---|---|---|
| | pre- | de- | pro- | ex- | mini- | inter- |
| | con- | re- | un- | sub- | ultra- | extra- |

| Suffixes: | -fy | -ish | -en | -less | -ous | -ship |
|---|---|---|---|---|---|---|
| | -able | -ing | -al | -ness | -ize | -like |
| | -ly | -ed | -er | -ment | -hood | -ward |

# WHO'S WHO

Review with your class the meaning of the suffix "-ist" and then call out the following occupations. Ask your students to tell what each person would study. If they don't know the answer, tell them. Repeat the activity frequently and watch them learn!

| | | |
|---|---|---|
| **ichthyologist** | **zoologist** | **podiatrist** |
| **fish** | **animals** | **feet** |
| **anthropologist** | **botanist** | **pharmacist** |
| **man** | **plants** | **drugs** |
| **economist** | **audiologist** | **entomologist** |
| **money** | **hearing** | **insects** |
| **agronomist** | **hydrologist** | **etymologist** |
| **soil** | **water** | **words** |

# MAD SCRAMBLE

Write one or two of your class's current spelling words on the board. Ask students to scramble the letters to make new words. They may use all or only some of the letters. Give them three or four minutes to work. Then ask one student to read his or her list. As the list is read aloud, other students with the same words should cross them off their lists. Students may score one point for each word they made that wasn't read from the first list.

A variation:
Select one spelling word. Do not write it on the board. Instead, write two or three words that could also be made with those letters. See if students can decide which spelling word you selected.

# MAKE IT MORE

Students in all grades need constant review and practice in making singular words plural.

Give students singular words and ask them to pronounce and spell their plural forms. You may also ask students to name the rule being followed in making the plural. (Save irregular plurals for a separate drill.)

Some words to start with:

| | | | | |
|---|---|---|---|---|
| potato | valley | city | box | child |
| solo | knife | day | shelf | mouse |
| guess | story | book | boy | tomato |
| county | dish | half | monkey | woman |
| leaf | penny | dime | key | son-in-law |
| cry | bubble | bench | pencil | bus |

# TWO BY TWO

Have students practice thinking of things that come in twos or pairs. Ask each student to name something that is found or bought two-at-a-time. (Some things are a single item but are called a pair.)

Examples:

| | | |
|---|---|---|
| a pair of pajamas | socks | eyes |
| a pair of earrings | scissors | ears |
| arms | twins | jeans |
| legs | lollipops | long johns |
| shoes | handcuffs | glasses |

# SNAP IT!

Call out one of the words listed below. Ask students to "snap out" another word that can be combined with your word to make a compound word. Students should provide as many combinations as possible before going on to the next word.

| | | | | |
|---|---|---|---|---|
| class | line | eye | yard | board |
| read | shake | out | lid | book |
| camp | in | side | out | man |
| hand | junk | some | boy | foot |
| door | week | end | time | town |
| day | every | room | air | water |

# POSITIVE AND NEGATIVE WORDS

Sometimes two words mean almost the same thing, but elicit different feelings when they are used.

Read each word pair listed below and let students decide which word is more likely to cause negative feelings.

| | |
|---|---|
| cheap / inexpensive | dumb / ignorant |
| thin / skinny | thrifty / cheap |
| chubby / fat | nosy / curious |
| sly / sneaky | enthusiastic / rowdy |
| clever / tricky | timid / shy |

# ABC WORD GAMES

Choose a category from this list. Have students think of words in that category that start with each of the letters of the alphabet. Call on the first student to give an appropriate word that starts with "A" and then continue around the class. Any student who cannot think of a word for his or her turn may be skipped. Come back to those students after each student has had a chance to answer or on the next round.

Sample categories:

| | |
|---|---|
| proper nouns | compound words |
| common nouns | hyphenated words |
| adjectives | five-letter words |
| adverbs | words that mean "said" |

# PRO OR CON?

Read one of the statements listed below. Select one student to speak for the idea and one student to speak against the idea. Give each student about one minute to speak. Then ask the rest of the class with which side they agree (by a show of hands).

✦ **From now on, trees should not be cut down.**

✦ **Each person should drive as fast or as slowly as he or she thinks is safe.**

✦ **Families should be allowed to have a limited number of appliances that require electricity.**

✦ **Children should be encouraged to use the Internet.**

✦ **Medical care should be offered free of charge to everyone in this country.**

# ATTENTION: ACROSTICS

Print a word on the board vertically. You may choose from the list of "substantial" words given below or provide your own.

**Liberty        Achievement        Friendship        Conservation**

Instruct students to write an acrostic poem by writing one sentence that starts with each letter of the word.

Example:

**L**iberty means accepting responsibility.
**I** am proud of my country.
**B**etsy Ross designed the flag.
**E**veryone is created equal.
**R**ed in the flag means courage.
**T**he liberty bell is located in Philadelphia.
**Y**ou should show respect for our flag.

# AD-WISE

Let students try their hands at advertising. Name one of the following items. Let students give as many brief advertising ideas as they can in five minutes for that item.

- ✦ **polka dot socks**
- ✦ **spicy toothpaste**
- ✦ **bubblegum-scented hairspray**
- ✦ **calendars without Mondays**
- ✦ **shoes that expand as your feet grow**
- ✦ **pocket-sized vacuum cleaners**
- ✦ **invisible eyeglasses**

# THINK ON YOUR FEET

Impromptu speaking gives students a chance to think on their feet. Select one of the subjects below. Call on one student to talk about the subject for about one minute. Select a different subject for the next student. Add other subjects to the list for future talks.

Suggested Subjects:
- ✦ **You are the basketball hoop in the school gymnasium. Describe your day.**
- ✦ **You are the principal of your school for today. What will you do?**
- ✦ **You are an Arctic tern making an amazing migration from the Arctic to the Antarctic. Tell about your trip.**
- ✦ **You will make all decisions about the school lunch menu. Tell us about your decisions.**

# STORY CHAIN

List one of the following word banks on the board. Explain that the class is going to compose a story together (orally). Each person will contribute just one sentence. Students use the word bank to help them compose the story. Remind the last people in the room that they will be responsible for bringing the story to an end. If a student seems "stuck" when it is his or her turn, come back to him or her later.

| Word Banks | #1 | #2 | #3 | #4 |
|---|---|---|---|---|
| | airplane | house | flowers | power failure |
| | blizzard | fun | bees | party |
| | hungry | fire | gift | emergency |
| | bear | stairs | race | panic |
| | trouble | twins | bouquet | hero |
| | crash | trapped | scream | friends |

# DECISIONS, DECISIONS

Let as many students as possible respond to the following situations:

You have just received $100 to spend on anything you want. How would your choice be affected if:

✦ **you had to spend it within the next hour?**

✦ **you couldn't spend it all in one place?**

✦ **you had to first keep it for three months?**

✦ **you had to spend it on something that would last at least five years?**

✦ **you had to spend it on something that wouldn't last more than a day?**

✦ **you had to spend it on someone else?**

# FORWARDS, BACKWARDS

Palindromes are words that read the same backwards as they do forwards. Give your students a few examples.

**pop**

**mom**

**anna**

**wow**

Have your students list as many palindromes as possible while you record them on the board. Challenge them to try palindromic phrases, such as, "I am, am I?" (a whole-word palindrome), or "Madam, I'm Adam" (a letter-by-letter palindrome).

# PROPERLY SPEAKING

To reinforce the difference between common and proper nouns, give students a common noun and ask them to name a proper noun in that category. (You may sometimes want to give proper nouns and let the students name the appropriate common noun.)

Sample common nouns:

| | | |
|---|---|---|
| movie | TV show | place |
| book | street | park |
| city | woman | holiday |
| man | state | president |
| month | day | river |

# SISTERS AND BROTHERS

Ask the students:

✦ **How many of you have younger sisters or brothers?**
✦ **What are some of the problems of being the older sister or brother?**
✦ **What are some of the advantages of being the older sister or brother?**

Ask the students who have older sisters and brothers to discuss some of the advantages and disadvantages of being younger siblings.

Let any of the students who are an only child tell what that is like.

# SLIMMING SUBJECTS

Students often find it difficult to begin writing a story or report because their topics are too broad.

Give students one of the broad topics listed below and ask them to suggest related topics that are more narrow.

Topics:

| | |
|---|---|
| **mammals** | **famous authors** |
| **airplanes** | **travel** |
| **basketball** | **tennis** |
| **music** | **painting** |
| **North America** | **trees** |
| **dogs** | **Africa** |

# PLASTIC MONEY

Most young adults are familiar with the use of credit cards, but they may not be aware of the advantages and disadvantages of using plastic money. Lead a discussion of the good and bad aspects of using credit cards.

GOOD
- ✦ **don't have to carry cash**
- ✦ **helpful in emergencies**
- ✦ **can buy now, pay later**
- ✦ **good identification**
- ✦ **helps you take advantage of unexpected good sales**

BAD
- ✦ **spend more than you make**
- ✦ **cards can be stolen and misused**
- ✦ **tempts you into impulsive buying**
- ✦ **makes spending too easy**
- ✦ **may ruin your credit if abused**

# THINK & FINISH

Analogies are great tools for sharpening thinking skills. An analogy shows relationships between words in two pairs of words. In each pair, the words must have the same relationship.

Review the concept of analogies with students. Point out the different kinds of relationships that show up in analogies (see below). Ask students to finish these analogies. They can also create their own analogies for classmates to finish. (A possible answer is given for each. There may be other correct ways to finish the analogy.)

| | | | |
|---|---|---|---|
| (synonym) | savory : tasty | as | boring :_____(dull) |
| (antonym) | novice : professional | as | _____ : slander (truth) |
| (degree) | _____ : scalding | as | cool : freezing (warm) |
| (function) | mitt : _____ | as | bat : hit (catch) |
| (location) | channel : television | as | _____ : radio (station) |
| (categories) | stomach : digestion | as | trachea : _____ (respiration) |
| (word structure) | unfriendliness : _____ | as | nonsensical : sense (friend) |
| (other) | _____ : operate | as | detective : investigate (surgeon) |

**Math**

Math

*Math*

Math

**Math**

Math

*Math*

Math

**Math**

# MYSTERY NUMBERS

Play this game to review number concepts and sharpen thinking skills. Ask students to find the mystery number (or numbers) that could fit each of the following descriptions. If time allows, let students describe their own mystery numbers for others to find.

✦ **I'm a 3-digit even number with a value greater than 500. Two digits are less than 5. There are no odd digits. The sum of my digits is 12. Who am I?**
(*Some possible answers*: 642, 624, 606, 822, 804, 840)

✦ **My last digit is 0. My first digit is 9. The sum of my digits is 25. I have four digits. Who am I?**
(*Some possible answers*: 9880, 9970, 9790)

✦ **I am a 3-digit number. The sum of my digits is 9. The product of my digits is 24. Who am I?**
(*Some possible answers*: 423, 342, 243)

# WHO'S THE WINNER?

Students will need to use logical thinking to determine the winner in the problems below. They may also need to draw a diagram.

If time permits, ask students to devise their own logic problems about races.

✦ **Four runners are at the end of a race. Lucy finished ahead of Sal but behind Amy. Jan beat Sal but not Lucy.**
**Who won the race? (Amy)**

Harder:
✦ **Five ocean swimmers competed in the race. Ike finished just ahead of Oscar. Felix finished later than Mike but ahead of Deke. Mike beat Ike. Oscar did not beat Felix.**
**Who won the race? (Mike)**

# PLACES, PLEASE!

Give students an opportunity to practice place value identification. Write one of the following numbers on the board. Ask students to name the value of a particular digit in that number. Select numbers based on the ability level of the students.

| Whole Numbers | 3456 | 103,103 |
|---|---|---|
| | 12,378 | 999 |

| Decimal Numbers | 12.342 | 99.999 |
|---|---|---|
| | .5602 | 103.103 |

Make up other numbers as you repeat the activity.

---

# NUMBER LINE-UP

Have each student jot down a two- or three-digit number on a sheet of paper. The numbers should be large enough for the entire class to see.

Ask students to stand up and display their numbers if they meet certain conditions as they are announced. Choose from the following ideas or make up other conditions.

+ a number under 100
+ a number that is a multiple of 5 (or 3, 6, etc.)
+ a number with digits that total to a certain sum
+ a number with digits that are in order from largest to smallest (765, etc.)
+ a number with digits that are all even numbers (244, 468, etc.)

# METRIC MADNESS

After students have learned metric measurement, try this activity for practice. List the units on the board in order from smallest to largest:

millimeter    centimeter    decimeter    meter    kilometer

Then ask students to decide if they would have to multiply or divide in order to change from:

- ✦ **millimeters to centimeters (divide by 10)**
- ✦ **kilometers to meters (multiply by 1000)**
- ✦ **centimeters to decimeters (divide by 10)**
- ✦ **decimeters to meters (divide by 10)**
- ✦ **meters to centimeters (multiply by 100)**
- ✦ **meters to kilometers (divide by 1000)**

# SIZE IT UP

This is a good measurement activity for a restless class. Give each student a ruler and ask them to find something in the classroom that is:

- ✦ **exactly one foot long**
- ✦ **less than six inches long**
- ✦ **two inches thick**
- ✦ **more than five inches wide**
- ✦ **half an inch wide**

Students can practice their metric measurement skills by measuring objects in centimeters, millimeters, and decimeters.

# OPERATIONS

Give students the examples below and ask them to tell you what operations must be used to arrive at the answers:

1) I start with 24 and end up with 27. (addition)
2) I start with 100 and end up with 10. (division by 10 or subtraction of 90)
3) I start with 144 and end up with 140. (subtraction)
4) I start with 3 and end up with 33. (addition of 30 or multiplication by 11)

Add other examples to the list or let students challenge each other with original examples. (The student thinking up the example gets just as much practice.)

# SIDE BY SIDE

Can your students name multi-sided closed figures?

Try these to find out:
- ✦ three-sided figure (triangle)
- ✦ four-sided figures (quadrilateral, rectangle, square, rhombus, parallelogram, trapezoid)
- ✦ five-sided figure (pentagon)
- ✦ six-sided figure (hexagon)
- ✦ seven-sided figure (heptagon)
- ✦ eight-sided figure (octagon)
- ✦ nine-sided figure (nonagon)
- ✦ ten-sided figure (decagon)
- ✦ twelve-sided figure (dodecagon)

# PRESIDENT'S MONEY

Can your students tell you which president's portrait is on each denomination of currency? Let them try to name them all.

| | |
|---|---|
| $1.00 | **Washington** |
| $5.00 | **Lincoln** |
| $10.00 | **Hamilton** |
| $20.00 | **Jackson** |
| $50.00 | **Grant** |
| $100.00 | **Franklin** |

Once students have learned which faces are on each denomination of currency, ask questions such as, "How much money do I have if I have one Washington and one Lincoln?" and "How much money do I have if I have one Franklin, two Grants, and a Jackson?"

# RACE TO 25

Students form two teams. The first member of Team A goes to the board and writes either "1" or "1 and 2." The first student from Team B goes to the board next and writes the next consecutive number or the next two consecutive numbers. The teams continue to alternate sending members to the board to write one or two consecutive numbers. The team whose member writes the number "25" on the board is the winner.

After you have completed this activity several times, ask students what strategies they are using. Does it seem to make a difference if both teams employ the same strategy? Can you control the results better by being the first team to play? Would the game be easier or harder if you could write three consecutive numbers?

# MOVING ON

Play this game to let students practice multiplication facts. Select one student to begin. That student should stand up next to the first student in the first row. Call out or display a flash card with a multiplication problem on it. The first of the two students to answer correctly gets to move on to the next student's desk. (If the seated student answers first, he or she trades places with the standing student.)

The student standing continues to move around the room as long as he or she answers correctly first. Any student who makes it back to his or her original starting position can be declared the winner!

# TRICKY NUMBERS

Tell students to follow your directions and you will guess the numbers they start with:

1. **Write down your favorite number.**
2. **Multiply the number by 4.**
3. **Add 20 to the product.**
4. **Divide the answer by 4.**

To find a student's mystery number, ask what the final answer was. Subtract five from this number. The result is the student's starting number.

After you have impressed them with your ESP, do a few examples on the board and trace the "magic" of the trick.

# NAME A UNIT

Name one of the following objects or actions and have students name the appropriate unit for measuring it:

- ✦ **time it takes to run six feet (seconds)**
- ✦ **bolts of fabric or ribbon (yards)**
- ✦ **width of a chocolate chip (millimeters or 16ths of an inch)**
- ✦ **amount of milk in a glass (ounces or milliliters)**
- ✦ **swinging of a pendulum (times per minute . . . a relationship as well as a unit is needed)**
- ✦ **distance between two cities (kilometers or miles)**
- ✦ **length of a pencil (inches or centimeters)**
- ✦ **area of a floor (square feet or square yards)**

---

# RELATED NUMBERS

Write several pairs of numbers on the board. Ask students to tell how all the pairs of numbers are alike or what relationship they share.

Examples:

- ✦ **6, 36       10, 100       15, 225**
  **(Each pair is the square root of a number and that number.)**

- ✦ **13, 19       55, 61       117, 123**
  **(Six has been added to the first number of each pair.)**

- ✦ **2, 18       3, 12       6, 6**
  **(The numbers of each pair are factors of 36.)**

- ✦ **2, 12       9, 99       3, 27**
  **(The second number of each pair is a multiple of the first number.)**

# EVEN STEVEN

Some things are not as easy to share "Even Steven" as other things. For instance, it's not as easy to share a bicycle as it is to share two quarters with another person. Ask your students to tell how they would share these things:

✦ **Four people must share a sandwich.**

✦ **You have rented a bicycle built-for-two for an hour. There are five of you paying for the bike. How do you share the bike?**

✦ **There are twelve new boxes of crayons, but thirty-six students in your class. How will your teacher have you share the crayons?**

✦ **There are nine people in your reading group, but the play has only six characters. What will you do?**

# EQUAL VALUES

Ask your students what would be an equal amount of money to:

✦ **3 quarters (7 dimes plus 1 nickel or 75 pennies)**

✦ **2 dollars (20 dimes or 40 nickels or 4 half-dollars)**

✦ **10 nickels (5 dimes or 50 pennies or 2 quarters)**

✦ **3 half-dollars (6 quarters or 15 dimes or 1 dollar and 2 quarters)**

✦ **2 quarters, 1 dime, and 1 nickel (65 pennies or 13 nickels or 4 dimes, 4 nickels, and 5 pennies)**

Make up other examples for students to practice money values.

# ADD ON

Separate the class into two teams. List the numbers 1-10 on the board. Choose a target number between 15 and 55. Let one member of the first team come to the board and select one of the listed numbers. Cross that number off of the list and write it on the board in another spot. Then let one member of the second team come to the board and cross out another number from the list. Add that amount to the first number that was selected. Continue to let members of each team come to the board, select a number from those remaining, and add it to the others. The team whose member hits a target number wins.

Example with a target of 23:
+ "Team A" chooses 3. "Team B" chooses 7. The total is 10.
+ "Team A" chooses 8. Total is 18. "Team B" chooses 5.
+ The total is now 23, the target number. "Team B" wins.

# DIGITS

Ask students to write a two-digit number in which:
+ **The sum of the digits is 12 (or any other amount).**
+ **The first digit is larger than the second.**
+ **There is a difference of 6 between the two digits.**
+ **One digit is the double of the other.**

Ask students to write three-digit numbers in which:
+ **All three digits are even (or all three digits are odd).**
+ **The number reads the same forwards and backwards.**
+ **The digits total a specific amount.**
+ **All of the digits are different and are written in a specified order (from largest to smallest or vice versa).**

Try other activities with four- and five-digit numbers.

# TALKING MATH

These sayings sound like they are about math or numbers. What do your students think? Ask them to explain the meanings of the following expressions:

✦ **Hang ten.**
✦ **Count me in.**
✦ **six in one, half dozen in the other**
✦ **It doesn't add up.**
✦ **cheaper by the dozen**
✦ **Take five.**
✦ **double or nothing**
✦ **one for the money, two for the show**

# DATED DIGITS

Roman numerals may not be in common use nowadays, but they still are part of everyday life. Students will run across them on clocks, on historical sites, in math lessons, in outlines, or in book introductions. Let students review their skills with converting Arabic numerals to Roman numerals. See how many of these dates they can "decipher" accurately in five minutes. Write the Roman numerals on the board one at a time.

| | | |
|---|---|---|
| MDXV . . . . . (1515) | CMLXXXII . . . (982) | MI . . . . . . . . (1001) |
| ML . . . . . . . . (1050) | MCMXCIX . . . (1999) | MMX . . . . . . (2010) |
| DCXIV . . . . . . . (614) | MMIII . . . . . . (2004) | MDCXLV . . . . (1645) |
| CCCXIII . . . . . . (313) | MMLX . . . . . (2060) | MX . . . . . . . . (1010) |
| MDCCCL . . . . (1850) | MCMLXXVI . . (1976) | MDXXXIX . . . (1539) |
| MCMI . . . . . . (1901) | DCCLXXVII . . . (777) | MDXXXVI . . . (1806) |
| MDCXXIX . . . (1629) | DLV . . . . . . . . . (555) | MCDXCII . . . (1492) |

# ON THE JOB

Brainstorm in small groups or as an entire class to see how many math-related jobs or careers students can think of in five minutes.

As a variation, think of careers that use specific math skills, such as:

- ✦ **counting money**
- ✦ **recording elapsed time**
- ✦ **estimating**
- ✦ **measuring**
- ✦ **tallying**

# SYMMETRY SEARCH

Have a symmetry search in your classroom. Ask students to find things in the room that have lines of symmetry.

As they identify objects with lines of symmetry, ask how many lines of symmetry each object has. Some objects have rotational symmetry (the object can be rotated and still have lines of symmetry in each position).

If you have access to small hand mirrors, let students examine the letters of the alphabet as they write them on the board or on paper. Do the letters look the same when reflected in the mirrors? Is the symmetry horizontal or vertical? Which letters have no lines of symmetry?

# STORY FACTS

Students are used to finding answers, not problems! Give students a set of facts and let them come up with a problem suitable for those facts.

Example:
  Two times four equals eight. (Fact)
  John bought two boxes of candy bars. Each box had four bars in it.
  How many candy bars did John have? (Problem)

**Other facts:**
  $100 - 87 = 13$
  $86 \div 2 = 43$
  $27 + 36 = 63$

Let students challenge each other with facts without problems.

# WHAT'S WRONG?

Write some problems on the board that have intentional errors in them. Forget to carry when adding, forget to change digits when borrowing, don't carry the correct digit when adding a column that totals to more than nine, and so on.

Challenge students to find the errors. Ask them to tell how the problems would be solved to arrive at the correct answers.

Or, write five problems and answers on the board. Let students find the one problem that is wrong and tell what is wrong with it.

*Being aware of common errors is helpful to students when proofing their own work.*

# BODY MATH

Let your students experience "Body Math." Have them use the width of their palms, the length of their feet, or the length of their pinky fingers as a standard unit by which to measure the:

✦ **width of the room,**
✦ **height of a chair,**
✦ **distance between desks, or**
✦ **any other distances in your classroom**

Discuss the results and how standardized units are necessary in order to accurately communicate measurements to others.

# TIME SENSE

This activity will help students develop a better sense of short periods of time.

Have students put their heads on their desks and close their eyes. Name a specific amount of time that you want them to wait (10 seconds, 45 seconds, 1 minute, 2 minutes, etc.). Instruct students to raise their hands when they think the specified amount of time has elapsed. Say "start" and begin timing silently.

When this exercise is repeated several times, your students will begin to more accurately estimate the measured passage of time.

# MENTAL MATH

Have students practice mental math skills and estimation at the same time. Explain that two numbers will be called out, one at a time. As each number is called, the class or an individual student, should respond with that number rounded to the nearest tens place. After both numbers have been called, the class or student should respond with the estimated total or difference, whichever is specified.

Example:

| Teacher: "23." | Student: "20." |
| Teacher: "47." | Student: "50." |
| Teacher: "Total?" | Student: "70." |

Students can then add or subtract the actual numbers on the board to see how close the estimation is to the actual sum or difference.

# YOUR OPINION COUNTS

Let your students discuss the following questions:
+ **How are the numbers 50 and 500 alike? How are they different?**
+ **What is your favorite two-digit number? Why is it your favorite?**
+ **Do you have a lucky number? What is it? Why do you think that it is lucky for you?**
+ **Are some multiplication facts more difficult to learn than others? Which ones? Are some easier?**
+ **Is it more difficult to learn to regroup in subtraction or in addition?**
+ **What is your favorite math activity?**

# MATH WORD CHALLENGE

Challenge students to know their math vocabulary. Call out one of the words listed below and ask for a volunteer to explain its meaning. Any student who disagrees can challenge the definition and correct it.

| | | |
|---|---|---|
| vertex | factor | quadrilateral |
| perimeter | product | multiple |
| area | quotient | prime number |
| fraction | sum | composite number |
| equivalent | divisor | circumference |
| numerator | ray | diameter |
| denominator | line | square |

See additional math terms on the Math Terms card below.

# MATH TERMS

Challenge students further with these math terms (including some computer lingo):

| | | |
|---|---|---|
| binary | absolute value | closed figure |
| byte | addend | Cartesian set |
| RAM | axis | cardinal number |
| decagon | cube | complex fraction |
| circumference | remainder | mean |
| pi | prime | ratio |
| square root | transversal | bit |

# PRODUCING PATTERNS

Write a number pattern on the board. Let students decide the pattern of that particular group of numbers:

Example:

| | | |
|---|---|---|
| 2  4  6  8  10 | ...................... | **Pattern: increase by 2** |
| 1  3  2  4  3  5  4 | ........... | **Pattern: increase by 2, decrease by 1** |
| 1  2  4  8  16 32 | ................. | **Pattern: double each number** |
| 5  10 15 20 25 30 | ................ | **Pattern: consecutive multiples of 5** |
| 25 24 20 19 15 14 10 | ........... | **Pattern: decrease by 1, decrease by 4** |

---

# TWELVE QUESTIONS

Select a number from 1 to 100. Write it on a slip of paper so that it can be shown to students later.

Let students ask questions that can be answered with "yes" or "no." Their goal is to discover the number in twelve questions or less. As an alternate activity, count only those questions that result in a "no" response.

After a few rounds of questions, discuss the types of questions that help narrow down the choice of numbers:

✦ **Is it an even number?**
✦ **Is it greater than 50? Less than 50?**
✦ **Is the first digit larger than the second digit (if it is a two-digit number)?**

# BONKERS

Ask your students to count aloud by ones as you go around the room. Before you start, select a set of multiples (example: multiples of 3).

Whenever a student's turn lands on a multiple of the selected number, the student says "Bonkers!" instead of the number. Encourage the students to go as quickly as they can.

Example:
**All multiples of 3 are "Bonkers." Students count as follows: 1, 2, Bonkers, 4, 5, Bonkers, 7, 8, Bonkers, and so on.**

To increase the complexity (and the fun), select two numbers whose multiples are to be "Bonkers" at the same time (for instance, 3 and 4).

---

# PLACE IT

Have students draw 3 or 4 lines on a sheet of paper to be used as blank spaces. (Everyone should have the same number of blank lines.) Then call out a corresponding number of digits, one at a time. As you call out each one, the students should write it on one of their spaces in any order they choose. When you have finished calling out all the digits, ask students to share the numbers they constructed. List these combinations on the board. What is the largest number possible? The smallest number possible? What numbers could be made that fall between the largest and smallest?

To change this activity a little bit, tell students to try to make the largest (or smallest) number possible. However, chance is part of this activity. Students may not change the position of a digit once it is written on their papers.

(The students will consider it more fair if you write the digits 0 to 9 on cards and pull them at random.)

# FACTOR FRENZY

Separate the class into two teams.

Call out a number. Let the teams alternate naming a factor of that number. The last team to name a factor scores a point. The other team answers first on the next number. Continue until one team has 10 points.

If your students are really good at finding factors, try a more difficult activity. Write two numbers (between 0 and 12) on the board. Have students name numbers that have both of those numbers as factors.

Example:
**2 and 9 are the numbers you name.**
**18, 36, 54, 72 are all numbers that have both 2 and 9 as factors.**

# WORTHY WORDS

List the letters of the alphabet on the board with a number value for each (A = 1, B = 2, C = 3 . . . Z = 26).

Ask students:
- ✦ **to make up words with a certain value (a value of 7: BAD, BE, DAB).**
- ✦ **to calculate the total value of a certain word (ARITHMETIC = 106).**
- ✦ **to calculate the value of their own names.**
- ✦ **If letters cost the same as their point values (A = 1 cent), what words could they buy for a nickel? A dime? A quarter? A dollar?**
- ✦ **If they can make a sentence using only nickel words, what would those words be?**

# STATE THE PROBLEM

Give students an answer. Let them give as many problems as possible to "fit" the answer.

Complicate the activity by requiring that the problems involve a specific operation (addition, subtraction, multiplication, or division).

If you have a longer period of time, separate the class into two teams. Call out the answer. Then alternate between the two teams, letting each give problems for that answer. If a team cannot think of another problem, the other team scores a point and gives the first response to the next answer.

# TELL HOW

State a math task. Let students tell how to accomplish it.

Examples:
- ✦ **Find the area of a square. (Multiply the length of a side by itself and express in square units.)**
- ✦ **Convert minutes to seconds. (Multiply by 60.)**
- ✦ **Find the perimeter of a figure. (Add all the sides.)**
- ✦ **Find the circumference of a cylinder when the diameter is known. (Multiply the diameter by 3.14.)**
- ✦ **Find an equivalent fraction for a given fraction. (Multiply the denominator and the numerator by the same number.)**
- ✦ **Convert feet to inches. (Multiply by 12.)**
- ✦ **Convert quarters to dollars. (Divide by 4.)**

# IT'S A BARGAIN

Anytime that a quality item can be purchased below the normal price, it's a bargain. Some sales that are supposed to be great bargains really aren't.

Let students decide which of the following sale prices are really bargains:

| | |
|---|---|
| ✦ **Candy bars 40¢ each** | **Sale 3/$1.00 (Bargain)** |
| ✦ **Wacky shoelaces 75¢ a pair** | **Sale 2 pairs/$1.00 (Bargain)** |
| ✦ **Pencils 10¢ each** | **Sale 3/25¢ (Bargain)** |
| ✦ **Comic books 50¢ each** | **Sale 6/$3.50 (Not a bargain)** |

Add other items to the list this activity is repeated.

# MONEY OFF

Many times sale prices are not directly listed. Instead, the ticket or sign will indicate an amount to be taken off the normal price.

Let the students practice computing the sale price when you give the normal price and the amount to be taken off. To really sharpen their skills, practice this activity two or three times a week for a few minutes at a time using different amounts.

| | |
|---|---|
| **Jeans $18.00** | **½ off ($9.00)** |
| **Shoes $25.00** | **⅕ off ($20.00)** |
| **Video game $20.00** | **¼ off ($15.00)** |
| **Gold chain $40.00** | **½ off ($20.00)** |
| **Record album $9.00** | **⅓ off ($6.00)** |
| **Board game $12.00** | **⅙ off ($10.00)** |

# PROFIT OR LOSS?

Let students do some mental arithmetic as they try to determine whether a profit or a loss was realized on each of the following transactions:

1. **You bought 8 oranges for 10¢ each and sold them 8 for $1.00. (Profit)**
2. **You bought a bike for $59.00, added a new tire to it for $10.00, then sold it for $75.00. (Profit)**
3. **You bought 3 books at a garage sale for a total of $2.00. Later you sold one to your brother for 75¢. Then you sold the others to your best friend for 50¢ each. (Loss)**
4. **You spent $5.50 to buy seeds, fertilizer, and flower pots. Only 3 pots of marigolds actually grew. You sold each pot of flowers for $1.50. (Loss)**

Let students bring in profit or loss problems for the class to solve.

---

# THE BEST DEAL

Divide students into 4 teams. Give one problem to each team. Compare the answers to decide who paid the smallest price for the total purchase.

Problem 1:  George bought a DVD player that was originally $92.50. He got a 45% discount and paid 8% in sales tax.

Problem 2:  Betsy got a 15% discount on some hats she just loved. She bought four of them! The original price was $19 each. She had to pay 5% in sales tax.

Problem 3:  Rufus bought a pet monkey at a 75% discount. Before the sale, the monkey's price was $169. Rufus paid no tax.

Problem 4:  Suzie headed for the hamburger sale. She took nine friends. The $2.50 burgers were on sale at a 25% discount. Each person (including Suzie) got two burgers. Suzie paid 6% tax and left a tip equal to 15% of the total price of the burgers (without the tax).

**Who paid the least?** (Rufus)

**Social Studies**

Social Studies

*Social Studies*

Social Studies

**Social Studies**

Social Studies

*Social Studies*

Social Studies

**Social Studies**

Social Studies

# BEAT THE CLOCK

Track down physical features on Earth's surface and polish map skills at the same time. Divide students into groups of about 3-5 students. Give each group an atlas and one of these lists. (The same list can be given to more than one group.) Ask them to find one example on Earth of each feature on the list and write down its proper name.

| | | | | |
|---|---|---|---|---|
| 1. gulf | 1. archipelago | 1. mountain | 1. island | 1. mountain range |
| 2. fjord | 2. lake | 2. cape | 2. volcano | 2. peninsula |
| 3. sea | 3. strait | 3. channel | 3. reef | 3. lagoon |
| 4. canal | 4. bay | 4. canyon | 4. harbor | 4. plain |
| 5. isthmus | 5. basin | 5. swamp | 5. desert | 5. delta |

Find a later time when groups can show the rest of the class the locations of the features on a large world map.

# RIGHT COUNTRY, WRONG CITY

Students will need to do some quick thinking to master this review of world cities. Tell them that you will read a group of five cities. All of the cities but one are from the same country. After you read the city names, students must identify the country AND name the city that does not belong with the group.

✦ Geneva, Lyon, Grenoble, Toulouse, Paris     (France, Geneva)

✦ Nanchung, Shanghai, Hanoi, Beijing, Nanjing     (China, Hanoi)

✦ Madrid, Acapulco, Xtapa, Cancun, Cabo San Lucas     (Mexico, Madrid)

✦ Florence, Venice, Barcelona, Naples, Milan     (Italy, Barcelona)

✦ St. Petersburg, Kiev, Moscow, Prague, Smolensk     (Russia, Prague)

✦ Madras, Cairo, Calcutta, Delhi, Bombay     (India, Cairo)

✦ Montreal, Anchorage, Calgary, Winnipeg, Toronto     (Canada, Anchorage)

✦ Oslo, Munich, Dusseldorf, Berlin, Frankfurt     (Germany, Oslo)

✦ Manchester, Birmingham, Oxford, London, Brussels     (England, Brussels)

✦ Nagano, Singapore, Kyoto, Tokyo, Osaka     (Japan, Singapore)

# WESTWARD HO!

List the following modes of transportation on the board. Let students put them in chronological order. Discuss how each mode has contributed to the development of this country.

| | |
|---|---|
| **steamboat** | **automobile** |
| **airplane** | **space shuttle** |
| **train** | **canoe** |
| **covered wagon** | **horse** |

What types of transportation do the students think might contribute to the future exploration of this country and of outer space?

---

# COMMUNICATIONS

Students will name spoken and written language as our main means of communication, yet we share our thoughts, feelings, and values in many other ways. See if your students can think of other ways in which we communicate.

Examples:
**music**
**clothing styles**
**dance**
**paintings, sculptures, and other art forms**
**religious ceremonies**
**plays, television, movies**

# LOOK AT THE USA

Let students open their social studies books to a map of the United States. Use this activity to give them practice finding features and places on the map.

- ✦ **Find our state.**
- ✦ **Name and locate a major chain of mountains.**
- ✦ **Name and locate at least two lakes and rivers.**
- ✦ **Name and locate some islands.**
- ✦ **Name and locate a peninsula.**
- ✦ **Find and name all the states that border our state.**

List additional activities on the back of this card for future use.

---

# BOUNTIFUL RESOURCES

Our country is blessed with many rich resources.

List the letters of the alphabet down the side of the chalkboard and let students try to name a resource that starts with each letter.

Example:
   **A = Apple orchards**
   **B = Birds**
   **C = Coal**
   **D = Deer**

Try to name only natural items. Do not include artificial products.

# SIGHTS TO SEE

Historic landmarks can be found all across the United States. Name some of the following sites. Ask if any student in your class has seen them. Let any student that has visited the site tell the class about it for a minute.

- ✦ **Mount Rushmore located in South Dakota (four presidents carved on the side of the mountain: Washington, Jefferson, Lincoln, T. Roosevelt)**
- ✦ **Statue of Liberty located in New York Harbor**
- ✦ **The Lincoln Memorial located in Washington, D.C.**
- ✦ **The Tomb of the Unknown Soldier located in Arlington, Virginia**
- ✦ **The Liberty Bell located in Philadelphia**

What other historic landmarks have your students visited or read about?

# NAME ANOTHER

Instruct your students to open their social studies books to a map of an area that they have studied.

Name a particular item by its proper name. Then ask the students to name another of the same item.

Example: (Looking at the USA map: Teacher, "Rio Grande River." Students, "Hudson River.")

You may want to name:

| | | |
|---|---|---|
| rivers | cities | highways |
| mountain ranges | lakes | countries |
| states | oceans | continents |

# AD-VICE

Divide the class into four teams. Assign each team a different advertising medium: radio, TV, newspaper, or billboard. Announce that you have just created a wonderful new candy. You are willing to spend all your advertising budget on one type of advertising.

Let the teams brainstorm for two minutes to think of as many reasons as possible why your candy should be advertised through their medium. They may also list disadvantages of the other advertising methods.

Give each team one minute to share their reasons with the class. Then have the students vote for the type of advertising that makes the most sense for the product. Don't let students vote for their own advertising.

Repeat this activity another time using a different product.

# IN DEMAND

Remind students how the law of supply and demand works:
**When demand is high, supply decreases and value increases.**
**When demand is low, supply increases and value decreases.**

Ask students to name examples of this law based on their own experiences. How many of them were unable to purchase a particular compact disc that was on the top ten list when they wanted it?

Other Examples:
**During the Christmas season, certain toys are in great demand. The latest video games, new dolls, electronic devices, and certain styles of clothing are hard to find. Later when their popularity fades, these items are sold at drastically reduced prices.**

# JOBS! JOBS! JOBS!

New products mean more jobs. Have students trace the production of one of these products from beginning to end, naming all of the jobs that are associated with its production and its distribution to consumers.

| | |
|---|---|
| pair of tennis shoes | soft drink |
| automobile | textbook |
| bicycle | pair of eyeglasses |
| pair of designer jeans | greeting card |
| candy bar | Christmas tree |
| movie | pencil |
| video game | musical album |

# BEST FOOT FORWARD

Discuss competition for jobs. A good example is the number of teenagers applying for summer jobs at fast food restaurants. Let students share their ideas of how job applicants can "put their best foot forward" when applying for a job. Some ideas to consider:

✦ attention to personal hygiene
✦ manner of speaking
✦ appropriate clothing
✦ handwriting and spelling on application form
✦ confidence and poise during interview
✦ interest in job responsibilities
✦ presentation of previous experience
✦ letters of recommendation

# WORTHY WORKERS

Compensation is not always commensurate with the services provided by workers. List or name the following jobs and services. Ask students to rank them according to the amount they should be paid (from lowest to highest salary):

| | |
|---|---|
| teacher | secretary |
| law enforcement officer | brain surgeon |
| garbage collector | author |
| professional athlete | bus driver |
| firefighter | rock musician |
| movie star | computer programmer |

Let students discuss why they ranked the jobs as they did.

# CONTINENTAL QUIZ

To help students become more familiar with the continents and to give them an opportunity to use globes, ask them these questions. If you have globes, let groups of students look at them for three to five minutes while you ask:

✦ **Does the equator pass through Africa?**
✦ **Why could we call Europe and Asia Eurasia?**
✦ **Are North and South America connected by land?**
✦ **Is Antarctica north of Europe?**
✦ **Are Africa and Australia connected by land?**

Let students ask questions of the rest of the class.

# BRAIN POWER

Remind students that most jobs have certain skill or knowledge requirements. Some jobs require more education than others.

Let students name specific jobs that fit into the following educational requirement categories:

+ **no education at all**
+ **less than high-school diploma**
+ **high-school diploma**
+ **college degree**
+ **specialized training (may or may not include a college education)**

# CONSUMER OR PRODUCER?

Our country enjoys a free enterprise system. People who make things are called producers. People who buy and use things are called consumers. Let your students tell which they would be if they:

+ **bought a transformer toy at the mall.**
+ **made french fries at a fast food restaurant.**
+ **operated a lemonade stand in your neighborhood.**
+ **bought a movie ticket.**
+ **went to the barbershop for a haircut.**
+ **created original Christmas cards for friends.**
+ **purchased new school supplies.**

# THOUGHTS OF FREEDOM

Discuss the Statue of Liberty and its history. Call on individual students to explain what the word "freedom" means to them.

Ask your students to distinguish between small and large freedoms as you call on different students to finish the sentence, "Freedom is to be able to . . ."

Examples:
- ✦ . . . vote on election day.
- ✦ . . . choose what kind of sandwich I want for lunch.
- ✦ . . . spend my own money on whatever I want.
- ✦ . . . decide what kind of job I want.

# RESOURCE DILEMMA

We are constantly making choices about the use of our natural resources. Students should be aware of the variety of ways in which we can use our resources. As adults they will be making decisions that will affect future generations.

Ask students to name ways that each of the following resources could be used and to decide which uses are most important or appropriate.

- ✦ **A river: to harness for electricity, to use for transportation, to use for recreational activities, to fish commercially**
- ✦ **An uninhabited piece of land: to use as a park, to build houses, to set aside as a nature preserve, to build a parking lot, to zone for commercial buildings**
- ✦ **A large area of timberland: to cut trees for lumber, to partially clear for a park, to cut trees for houses, to leave as a natural preserve**

# JUMBLED STATES

Give your students one of the jumbled state names listed below and let them "unjumble" it. You might want to keep track of their record times.

| | | |
|---|---|---|
| Alabama — Balmaaa | Kentucky — Centkkuy | North Dakota — Aaootkdthrn |
| Alaska — Sklaaa | Louisiana — Aaiiousnl | Ohio — Iooh |
| Arizona — Ziranoa | Maine — Aeinm | Oklahoma — Aaooklhm |
| Arkansas — Ssaaknra | Maryland — Aadlnmry | Oregon — Ooegnr |
| California — Aafciirnol | Massachusetts — Acaesstthumss | Pennsylvania — Aaiennspylvn |
| Colorado — Acdlooor | Michigan — Achigmni | Rhode Island — Aioedhrsndl |
| Connecticut — Nccoienttuc | Minnesota — Aeimnostn | South Carolina — Aaoouicsthrln |
| Delaware — Adaeelrw | Mississippi — Iiiippsssssm | South Dakota — Aauootkdhts |
| Florida — Afdirlo | Missouri — Iissrmou | Tennessee — Eeeessnnt |
| Georgia — Aeiggor | Montana — Aantomn | Texas — Aetsx |
| Hawaii — Aaihwi | Nebraska — Aaebksrn | Utah — Ahut |
| Idaho — Adioh | Nevada — Aadenv | Vermont — Eotnmrv |
| Illinois — Siiillno | New Hampshire — Aeeihpnwmsrh | Virginia — Aiingrvi |
| Indiana — Aadiinn | New Jersey — Eeewrjsyn | Washington — Aiontgnhsw |
| Iowa — Aiow | New Mexico — Eecionmwx | West Virginia — Estwaiiingrv |
| Kansas — Aakssn | New York — Eoykrwn | Wisconsin — Iiowscnsn |
| | North Carolina — Aaionorthcrln | Wyoming — Gioynmw |

# CAPITAL CATCH

Call out the name of a state in the USA, and ask the students to name the state's capital. Play this game at least once a week until students learn all of the states and their capitals.

| | | |
|---|---|---|
| Alabama—Montgomery | Kentucky—Frankfort | North Dakota—Bismarck |
| Alaska—Juneau | Louisiana—Baton Rouge | Ohio—Columbus |
| Arizona—Phoenix | Maine—Augusta | Oklahoma—Oklahoma City |
| Arkansas—Little Rock | Maryland—Annapolis | Oregon—Salem |
| California—Sacramento | Massachusetts—Boston | Pennsylvania—Harrisburg |
| Colorado—Denver | Michigan—Lansing | Rhode Island—Providence |
| Connecticut—Hartford | Minnesota—St. Paul | South Carolina—Columbia |
| Delaware—Dover | Mississippi—Jackson | South Dakota—Pierre |
| Florida—Tallahassee | Missouri—Jefferson City | Tennessee—Nashville |
| Georgia—Atlanta | Montana—Helena | Texas—Austin |
| Hawaii—Honolulu | Nebraska—Lincoln | Utah—Salt Lake City |
| Idaho—Boise | Nevada—Carson City | Vermont—Montpelier |
| Illinois—Springfield | New Hampshire—Concord | Virginia—Richmond |
| Indiana—Indianapolis | New Jersey—Trenton | Washington—Olympia |
| Iowa—Des Moines | New Mexico—Santa Fe | West Virginia—Charleston |
| Kansas—Topeka | New York—Albany | Wisconsin—Madison |
| | North Carolina—Raleigh | Wyoming—Cheyenne |

# NATIVE AMERICAN KNOW-HOW

The first Americans made many valuable contributions to our country. List three headings on the board:

**food and plants**              **medicines**              **inventions**

Explain that the following are contributions made by Native Americans. Ask students to tell which heading each contribution belongs under:

| | | | |
|---|---|---|---|
| **pipe** | **peanuts** | **quinine** | **moccasins** |
| **dog sled** | **cotton** | **petroleum jelly** | **pumpkin** |
| **corn** | **squash** | **canoe** | **hammock** |
| **witch hazel** | | | **popcorn** |

Can your students add other Native American contributions to the list?

---

# INVENTION MATCH

Name a famous inventor and ask the students to name the correct invention. Or, name the invention and let the students name the inventor responsible.

- ✦ **Benjamin Franklin** ...................................lightning rod
- ✦ **Alexander Graham Bell** ..........................telephone
- ✦ **Samuel Morse** ........................................telegraph
- ✦ **Wright Brothers** ....................................first successful airplane
- ✦ **Clarence Birdseye**.................................frozen food process
- ✦ **Thomas Edison** ......................................light bulb, phonograph
- ✦ **Elisha Graves Otis** .................................elevator
- ✦ **Jonas Salk** ..............................................polio vaccine

# OLDER OR BETTER?

Most products are worth more when they are new than when they are old, but that is not true of all items. Some products increase in value if they are kept a long time (especially if they remain in good condition).

Have students name items that they think will increase in value if they are kept for a long time. This list will help them get started:

**well-made furniture
paintings by famous artists
comic books
rare books/first editions
baseball cards
newspaper editions with significant historical headlines
cosmetic bottles
letters from famous people**

# TIME MACHINE

Tell students to pretend that they can climb into a time machine and go backward or forward in time. They will always land in the same place, just in a different time. Let them take turns describing their trips into the past or the future. Ask:

✦ **What does the area look like?**

✦ **How are the people dressed?**

✦ **What work do you see people doing?**

✦ **How are people traveling during this time?**

✦ **What do you notice that is most different from present time?**

Use this activity once a week and allow the students to research the time to which they want to travel.

# POLLUTION PATROL

Encourage students to be aware of local litter and pollution problems. Ask them to name some of the local recreational areas and to think about the kinds of litter they have seen in those places.

What can individuals do at the local level to stop pollution of their community environment? Discuss community programs that are aimed at curbing litter and pollution.

What is being done at your school to stop littering? Ask students to look out for litter they see as they move around the school campus. Are there ways they can help? Can they make posters? Do trash cans need to be put in more spots? Discuss what the class can do.

# PEACE LINKS

Our students will be responsible for world peace in the future. Discuss these questions with them for a few minutes:

- ✦ **Why do you think peace is important?**
- ✦ **Why do you think peace is difficult to achieve?**
- ✦ **How can you begin to prepare for your role in the future of world peace? (Discuss the importance of learning about other countries and their people.)**
- ✦ **What can we do now to help us learn about other parts of the world?**

# WHAT IS IT?

Use this quiz to help students practice map and globe skills.
Ask volunteers to define each of the terms listed below:

**Key:**          **tells what the symbols on a map represent**

**Legend:**       **tells what the symbols on a map represent**

**Scale:**        **tells what each measured unit of distance on the map stands for in real distance**

**Longitude:**    **imaginary lines that run east and west on the earth's surface**

**Latitude:**     **imaginary lines that run north and south on the earth's surface**

**Equator:**      **imaginary line that runs around the center of the earth, separating the north and south hemispheres**

# LEGENDARY LEARNING

Ask students to imagine they are going to make a map of their city.
Give them the following words and let them volunteer to come to the
board and draw a symbol for that object as if it were going to be used
on the map legend.

If a longer period of time is available, let each student make a complete
set of symbols for a legend on his or her own paper.

| | |
|---|---|
| **tree** | **day-care center** |
| **school building** | **sports field** |
| **house** | **restaurant** |
| **playground** | **airport** |
| **store** | **library** |
| **office building** | **grocery store** |

# IT'S CUSTOMARY

Every country in the world has unique social customs. The United States has many customs that we might not even think about; they are a part of our everyday life. Ask your students to think of customs practiced in this country that might be done differently in other parts of the world.

Here are some to get them started:

- ✦ **shaking hands when meeting someone**
- ✦ **sending greeting cards at Christmas**
- ✦ **families eating meals together**
- ✦ **pledging allegiance to the flag in school each day**
- ✦ **filling baskets with colored eggs for Easter**

# UNIVERSAL SIGNS

We don't always have to speak the same language in order to communicate with people from other lands. There are many gestures and expressions that mean the same thing to all people. How many can your students name?

- ✦ **beckoning with a finger**
- ✦ **holding palm upright to mean "stop"**
- ✦ **putting one's finger to his or her lips to command silence**
- ✦ **shrugging shoulders to indicate puzzlement or uncertainty**
- ✦ **waving good-bye**
- ✦ **scratching one's head to indicate confusion or uncertainty**

# WEATHER WORRIES

Weather and climate play an important role in the way people live in various parts of the world. Discuss the difference between weather and climate.

Weather: the particular atmospheric conditions at any given time in a specific place

Climate: the overall year-round weather patterns of a particular place

Discuss:
- ✦ **What would happen if the earth's temperature began to increase constantly?**
- ✦ **What would happen if the amount of precipitation suddenly decreased?**
- ✦ **What would happen if we no longer had changes of seasons?**

# BE RESOURCEFUL

Our natural resources are invaluable to us. Many resources are in limited supply. We must use our resources carefully.

Name one of the resources listed below and let the students discuss ways it might be used. Encourage them to discuss problems that might occur from overuse or abuse of each resource. Which uses are most appropriate? What conflicts arise when choices have to be made? How should these decisions be made? Who controls each resource?
- ✦ **forest area**
- ✦ **natural gas**
- ✦ **ocean beach**
- ✦ **fossil fuels**
- ✦ **large rivers (such as the Mississippi)**

# STATES IN JEOPARDY

Ask the students to open their social studies books to a map of the United States. Using the Jeopardy game format, give the students an answer and let them call out the appropriate question.

Examples:

+ **This state is a peninsula. (What is Florida, Alaska?)**
+ **These states' borders form right angles where they meet. (What are Utah, Colorado, Arizona, and New Mexico?)**
+ **This state has the Rio Grande River as a border with a foreign country. (What is Texas?)**

Make up more answers based on the social studies map available to you.

# OLD GLORY

Discuss the pledge of allegiance to the flag with your students. Ask students to define each of these words:

+ **pledge: a promise**
+ **allegiance: loyalty**
+ **indivisible: unable to be divided**

Find out what your students know about "Old Glory:"

+ **What do the stars represent?**
+ **How many stars are there?**
+ **How many stripes are there?**
+ **What do the stripes represent?**

# COMMUNITY HELPERS

Ask the students to name various community helpers that provide goods or services for them. Select one from the list they name and discuss the consequences if that person were no longer available.

Some helpers students might name include:
- ✦ **doctors**
- ✦ **teachers**
- ✦ **mail delivery persons**
- ✦ **garbage collectors**
- ✦ **firefighters**
- ✦ **weather reporters (meteorologists)**
- ✦ **ministers, priests, rabbis**

# I NEED, I WANT

Discuss with students the basic needs of human beings. Use this activity to give them practice discriminating between needs and wants.

As each item is named, let students respond with "need" or "want." (If students are restless, let them stand up for "needs" and sit down for "wants."

| | | |
|---|---|---|
| **shelter** | **shoes** | **electric heater** |
| **ice-cream soda** | **stereo** | **soap** |
| **bathing suit** | **socks** | **underwear** |
| **visit to the doctor** | **candy bar** | **tennis lessons** |
| **trip to the amusement park** | **milk** | **sleeping bag** |
| **new toy** | **bed** | **fresh air** |
| **haircut** | **tape recorder** | **water** |

# LITTER TELLS!

Archeologists learn much by studying the remains of ancient civilizations. What will future archeologists learn about us by examining our litter? What kinds of things will they find when they dig up our ruins thousands of years from now?

Let your students make a list of the things that they think are characteristic of our society at the present time.

Some starters:

| | |
|---|---|
| tennis shoes | skateboards |
| soft drink cans | footballs |
| curling irons | televisions |
| computer joysticks | compact discs |

# MI CASA, SU CASA

Having a home or a shelter is a basic need of humans. Ask students to tell who might live in the following houses or shelters:

- ✦ adobe hut
- ✦ igloo
- ✦ barrack
- ✦ dormitory
- ✦ mansion
- ✦ tent
- ✦ The White House
- ✦ palace
- ✦ apartment

# ROBOT RIOT

Discuss what computers do now and what they may do in the future. Will they be able to do many of the little things we do for ourselves now?

Let students decide how robots or computers could be involved with some of the following daily activities. Would they want robots to do all of these things for them?

✦ **getting out of bed in the morning (robot pulls back covers, etc.)**
✦ **getting dressed for work or school**
✦ **brushing teeth, combing hair**
✦ **preparing meals**
✦ **doing homework, writing reports**
✦ **doing household chores, yard work**

---

# DAYS TO CELEBRATE

The significance of patriotic holidays often becomes obscured. Give the name of one of the following holidays or the special date. Let students tell why that date is a holiday. Why do we celebrate that date? Be sure to point out that some holidays have been changed by the federal government to fall on a Monday as a matter of convenience.

| | |
|---|---|
| **Lincoln's Birthday** | **February 12th** |
| **Washington's Birthday** | **February 22nd** |
| **Memorial Day** | **May 30th** |
| **Flag Day** | **June 14th** |
| **Independence Day** | **July 4th** |
| **Columbus Day** | **October 12th** |
| **Veterans Day** | **November 11th** |
| **Thanksgiving** | **4th Thursday of November** |

# THE RIGHT ORDER

Read each of the following lists of events in U.S. history. Give students one minute to arrange the events in chronological order. (Do not give the dates. These are included for your information.)

✦ **Boston Tea Party (1773); U.S. Constitution approved (1789); Founding of Massachusetts colony (1620); French & Indian War (1754-1763); Declaration of Independence (1776)**

✦ **Star Spangled Banner written (1814); Lewis & Clark expedition (1804-1806); California Gold Rush (1849); Louisiana Purchase (1803); colony of Georgia founded (1732)**

✦ **Panama Canal opens (1914); Civil War ends (1865); Erie Canal opens (1825); Charles Lindbergh flies solo across the Atlantic (1927); women get the right to vote (1920)**

✦ **Oregon Trail opens (1842); America enters World War I (1917); Korean War (1950-1953); Battle of Wounded Knee (1890); the Great Depression (1929)**

✦ **U.S. enters Vietnam War (1965); Watergate scandal (1972); John F. Kennedy becomes president (1960); U.S. war in Afghanistan (2001); atomic bombs dropped on Japan (1945)**

# TOUGH CHOICES

Every economic decision involves weighing benefits and consequences (negative outcomes or costs). Read the examples aloud to students, one at a time. Ask them to identify benefits and consequences for each choice made.

✦ **Lenny O'Coin had two job offers. The restaurant job schedule was 7-10 A.M. and 4-8 P.M. five days a week. The pay was $12 an hour with health insurance. The pet care job was for 30 hours a week at $9 an hour. He could set his own schedule. Lenny chose the pet care job.**

✦ **A banker, Mr. John deposit, spent $200 on food each month. He also spent a lot of time cooking, and hated it. (He was a terrible cook.) He decided to eat all his meals out. Now he spends over $300 a month on food.**

✦ **Harvey Kares belonged to a health club that costs $39 a month. Recently he learned about an organization that can feed a hungry child in the third world for $1 a day. Harvey now gives the money to the charity instead of belonging to the health club.**

# Science
## Science
### *Science*
## Science
# Science
## Science
### *Science*
## Science
# Science

# KNOW YOUR "OLOGIES!"

How many fields of science can your students correctly identify? Call out the name of a scientific field. Give students a few seconds to tell what is studied within that field.

- anthropology (cultures)
- archaeology (past cultures)
- astrology (planets & stars)
- bacteriology (bacteria)
- biology (living things)
- botany (plants)
- cardiology (heart function)
- climatology (climate)
- cytology (cells)
- ecology (environment)
- entomology (insects)
- geology (Earth's surface)
- herpetology (reptiles)
- histology (tissues)
- ichthyology (fish)
- meteorology (weather)
- microbiology (microorganisms)
- mineralogy (minerals)
- oncology (cancer)
- ornithology (birds)
- paleontology (prehistoric life)
- pathology (diseases)
- petrology (rocks)
- physiology (functions of organs and organisms)
- seismology (earthquakes)
- zoology (animals)

# DAZZLING DISCOVERIES

Who is responsible for these grand discoveries or inventions? Students can search their memories, consult with each other, or quickly check references to find the accomplishments that match the people.

- Alexander Graham Bell
- James Watt
- Eli Whitney
- Alexander Fleming
- Jonas Salk
- Edward Jenner
- Albert Einstein
- Hippocrates
- Watson & Crick
- Marie and Pierre Curie
- Thomas Edison
- Louis Pasteur
- George Washington Carver
- Robert Fulton
- Heinrich Hertz
- Isaac Newton

# WHICH CAME FIRST?

Review the history of science by asking students to order events in science. This will help them place events in the broad perspective of time, and think about the progress of scientific advancements. Read the items in each group. Then ask, "Which came first?" (You could also ask of each group, "Which came last?")

✦ launch of first space satellite; discovery of anesthetics; invention of the wheel*

✦ development of atomic energy; invention of the steam engine*; invention of computers

✦ invention of the telephone; beginning of irrigation*; first video tape recording

✦ discovery that Earth is round*; use of laser beams; discovery of electricity

✦ discovery of penicillin; invention of the jet engine; development of the microscope*

✦ invention of TV; discovery that blood circulates*; invention of electric light bulb

*Event followed by * came first in that group.*

# REAL-LIFE SCIENCE

Science is everywhere! Students often think of science as something that is done in the lab or classroom. It is important for them to realize how much science is a part of everyday life.

Divide the class into groups of 2-3 students. Give each group the name of a place such as one of these listed below. Ask them to take 5 minutes to write down ways that science shows up in that place. Find time later for students to add to and share their lists.

| | | |
|---|---|---|
| ✦ backpack | ✦ your bedroom | ✦ freeway |
| ✦ winter Olympics | ✦ running shoes | ✦ hospital |
| ✦ kitchen | ✦ bathroom | ✦ grocery store |
| ✦ football game | ✦ classroom | ✦ coffee chop |
| ✦ amusement park | ✦ school cafeteria | ✦ car wash |
| ✦ restaurant | ✦ skating rink | ✦ airport |

# WHAT CAUSED IT?

One of the major concepts found frequently in science is the relationship between cause and effect. Students need frequent practice examining events and determining causes and effects. Read each example to students. Tell them that this is an effect (or result) of some event or stimulus. Ask them to decide what cause might have produced this effect. (Answers will vary.)

- ✦ **Effect: The body produces antibodies.**      **Cause:_____**
- ✦ **Effect: Ice cubes melt in a glass of iced tea.**      **Cause:_____**
- ✦ **Effect: A rattlesnake vigorously rattles its tail.**      **Cause:_____**
- ✦ **Effect: A meteoroid becomes a meteor.**      **Cause:_____**
- ✦ **Effect: A turtle pulls its head into its shell.**      **Cause:_____**
- ✦ **Effect: Sand piles up into a dune.**      **Cause:_____**
- ✦ **Effect: A swimmer gets out of the water and shivers.**      **Cause:_____**
- ✦ **Effect: A river drops silt when it reaches the ocean.**      **Cause:_____**

# STICKY FEET

The relationship between form and function of objects is a major scientific concept. Often the form (shape, size, appearance, or color) of an object allows the object to serve a particular function or perform in a certain way. Give students a quick exercise in connecting form to function. For each object below, tell how the form contributes to the function.

*Form*      *Function*

- ✦ **A snail's foot is sticky.**      _____
- ✦ **Plant cells have sturdy walls.**      _____
- ✦ **A bobsled is shaped like a bullet.**      _____
- ✦ **The inner layer of bone is spongy.**      _____
- ✦ **A frog has a long, sticky tongue.**      _____
- ✦ **A duck's feet are webbed.**      _____
- ✦ **Human skin has pores.**      _____
- ✦ **The outer ear is shaped like a funnel.**      _____
- ✦ **Veins in the circulatory system have valves.**      _____

# SCIENCE IS CLASSY

Classification is an important process in science. Most objects and events in the natural world can be grouped (or classified) with others that have similarities.

Read these two groups to students (one group at a time). Ask them to suggest a way the items in the group could be classified. (There may be more than one correct answer.)

- ✦ **earthquake, volcano, erosion, hurricane, windstorm**
- ✦ **observing, measuring, predicting, inferring, hypothesizing**
- ✦ **lobster, scorpion, tarantula, beetle, mosquito, wasp**
- ✦ **hydrogen, oxygen, neon, nitrogen, argon**

Ask students to think of items (objects, processes, or events) that would fit into each of these classes:

- ✦ **seed plants**
- ✦ **compounds**
- ✦ **animals with 6 legs**
- ✦ **things that sink in fresh water**
- ✦ **forms of precipitation**
- ✦ **elements**

# SMART PLANNING

Science is all about asking questions and searching for answers. One important scientific process is that of designing an experiment that will answer a question. Pose the following problem for students.

The problem: Find a way to toss a raw egg a long distance without breaking it. Consider substances or methods that will protect the egg. Then ask students to design an experiment that describes a way to investigate and answer a question. Ask them to include:

- ✦ **a statement of a question to answer**
- ✦ **a list of equipment and supplies**
- ✦ **a hypothesis**
- ✦ **the steps to follow in the experiment**
- ✦ **the variable(s) that will change**
- ✦ **the variable(s) that will not change**
- ✦ **how you will show the results**
- ✦ **how you will know when you've found an answer**

# QUICK CONVERSIONS

Science and math have a special relationship. It is almost impossible to do scientific investigations without using math skills, particularly measurement. Ask students to practice working with units of measurement. Ask these questions to challenge students in making quick measurement conversions.

| | | |
|---|---|---|
| ✦ 40 pts.. . . . . . . . . . . . . . . | How many gal.? | **(5)** |
| ✦ 35,000 cm . . . . . . . . . . . . | How many km? | **(3.5)** |
| ✦ 16 g. . . . . . . . . . . . . . . . | How many mg? | **(16,000)** |
| ✦ 2640 ft.. . . . . . . . . . . . . . | How many mi.? | **(0.5 or 1/2)** |
| ✦ 176 oz. . . . . . . . . . . . . . . | How many lbs.? | **(11)** |
| ✦ 69 km.. . . . . . . . . . . . . . . | How many m? | **(69,000)** |
| ✦ 12 T . . . . . . . . . . . . . . . . | How many lbs.? | **(24,000)** |
| ✦ 3.6 kL . . . . . . . . . . . . . . . | How many L? | **(3600)** |
| ✦ 41/2 qts.. . . . . . . . . . . . . . | How many oz.? | **(144)** |
| ✦ 20 yds. . . . . . . . . . . . . . . | How many ft.? | **(60)** |
| ✦ 2 decades  . . . . . . . . . . . | How many yrs.? | **(20)** |
| ✦ 80 yds . . . . . . . . . . . . . . | How many in.? | **(280)** |

# JOIN THE PLANETS

Let students review the structure of the solar system by "becoming" a part of it. Make signs or labels that name different bodies in the solar system (See below.) Pin these labels on the students. Use one student for the Sun, one for Earth's Moon, and nine for the planets. The other students can be asteroids.

Ask students to use their own bodies to "stand in" for the solar system bodies, forming a human model of the solar system. Let students decide where the different bodies should be placed. Once in proper place, they can move in a way to represent the movement of solar system bodies.

| Labels: | | | |
|---|---|---|---|
| | **Sun** | **Mars** | **Pluto** |
| | **Moon** | **Mercury** | **Neptune** |
| | **Jupiter** | **Venus** | **Earth** |
| | **Saturn** | **Uranus** | **asteroid** (*make several of these*) |

# CELESTIAL CHARADES

Here's a quick game for reviewing the constellations. Students "perform" alone or in pairs to convey the name of a constellation to the class. Tell students they may use mime, hand signals, charade signals, or other body movements to communicate. The class must name the constellation (Latin name, common name, or both).

Some constellations to try:

| | | |
|---|---|---|
| **Hydra (Water Snake)** | **Cancer (Crab)** | **Aquarius (Water Carrier)** |
| **Ursa Major (Great Bear)** | **Gemini (Twins)** | **Libra (Scales)** |
| **Ursa Minor (Little Bear)** | **Orion (Hunter)** | **Lupus (Wolf)** |
| **Draco (Dragon)** | **Aires (Ram)** | **Cetus (Whale)** |
| **Cygnus (Swan)** | **Taurus (Bull)** | **Aquila (Eagle)** |
| **Lyra (Lyre)** | **Capricorn (Goat)** | **Big Dipper** |
| **Scorpius (Scorpion)** | **Pisces (Fish)** | **Little Dipper** |
| **Leo (Lion)** | **Pegasus (Winged Horse)** | |

# EXTRATERRESTRIAL LANGUAGE

Go on a treasure hunt for words to speak the language of outer space. Ask students to compile a list of all the "celestial" words they can find or think of in five minutes. Provide science textbooks, encyclopedias, dictionaries, an Internet access to help them in their search. Let them add to the list over the next several days. You might use this word bank as the basis for a writing activity, such as science fiction tales.

Examples:

| | | | |
|---|---|---|---|
| **solar** | **constellation** | **worm hole** | **universe** |
| **sun** | **streaking** | **black hole** | **Milky Way** |
| **planets** | **sunspots** | **orbit** | **supercluster** |
| **pulsar** | **meteor** | **moon** | **quasar** |
| **asteroids** | **meteorite** | **eclipse** | **nebula** |
| **corona** | **shooting star** | **lunar** | **galaxy** |
| **sunspots** | **coma** | **supernova** | **magnitude** |
| **luminous** | **comet** | **rocket** | **elliptical** |

# WHICH AGENT?

Review the definition of erosion (the wearing away and moving of Earth's surface material) and the different agents that cause erosion (wind, ice, gravity, ground water, and moving water). Read the following descriptions of changes in Earth's crust. Ask students to name the agent of erosion responsible for each example.

✦ **Large masses of rock plunge quickly downhill in a rock slide. (gravity)**
✦ **Huge deposits of silt collect at the mouth of a river. (moving water)**
✦ **A large moraine, full of rocks, dirt, and gravel, builds up at the edge of a valley. (ice)**
✦ **Sand and rocks are tossed up on the shoreline. (moving water)**
✦ **Stalactites and stalagmites form inside caves. (ground water)**
✦ **A huge pile of sand builds up against a clump of grass. (wind)**
✦ **Sinkholes form, causing ground and buildings to collapse. (moving water)**
✦ **Dirt and dust in the air carve patterns in the surface of a cliff. (wind)**
✦ **Rain fills cracks in rocks. In cold weather the water freezes and cracks the rocks open. (ice)**

# DEVIOUS WEATHER REPORTS

Challenge students to give weather reports that don't actually name the weather! Have groups take turns giving a weather report or prediction for a particular weather condition without using the actual word. (For instance, they could describe an upcoming thunderstorm, blizzard, hailstorm, fog, sleet, lightning, snow, frost, tornado, hurricane, drought, gale, cyclone, typhoon, cold front, or warm front.) Tell them they must describe the condition well enough that the rest of the class will know what weather to expect.

Examples:

**Tomorrow, expect periods when raindrops fall through a layer of air colder than 3° Centigrade.**

**Warning! Conditions exist where winds of speeds greater than 75 mph are developing over warm, tropical water.**

# MOVING EVENTS

Write the names of several Earth processes (such as those below) on individual scraps of paper. Place the paper slips in a hat or basket. Divide students into groups of 2 or 3. Pass the hat, allowing each group to draw a slip. Give the groups a few minutes to decide how they will describe the process to the class without using any words. They must only use body movements and gestures to demonstrate the process. Use small snatches of time later in the day or on other days for groups to demonstrate, while the rest of the class tries to identify the Earth process.

Examples of Earth processes:

- ✦ tide movements
- ✦ development of tsunami
- ✦ dormant volcano
- ✦ active volcano
- ✦ flood activity
- ✦ weather front formation

- ✦ earthquake
- ✦ aftershock
- ✦ wind erosion
- ✦ moon phases
- ✦ orbiting
- ✦ glacial action

- ✦ weathering
- ✦ geyser eruption
- ✦ ocean current
- ✦ uplifting
- ✦ movement along fault
- ✦ erosion by moving water

# PHYLUM PROFILES

Make copies of the following chart for students. Let them work in small groups for a quick brush-up on the characteristics of different animal phyla. To complete the chart, they must complete information to fill in the blank spaces for each phylum. When the chart is complete, they will have two animal names and two characteristics of the animals in the phylum.

| Phylum | Animal Example | Animal Example | Characteristic | Characteristic |
|---|---|---|---|---|
| Porifera | | | | |
| Coelenterates | | | | |
| Mollusks | | | | |
| Echinoderms | | | | |
| Arthropods | | | | |
| Chordates | | | | |

# THINK FAST!

Have a stopwatch handy! Group students in pairs. Tell the class that you will read labels of some categories within life science. They will have 15 seconds to write an example of name that matches your instructions. Set the stopwatch at 15 seconds for each of the 20 items. When the time is up, move onto the next item. Name. . .

+ a cell process
+ a part of a plant root
+ an example of tropism
+ a parasite
+ 2 plant processes
+ a stage of growth in a seed plant
+ 2 conifers
+ 5 sensory organs
+ 3 body systems

+ 2 different kinds of muscles
+ an example of a response
+ a kind of aerobic exercise
+ 2 examples of primary consumers
+ an animal that undergoes metamorphosis
+ a plant found in a rainforest biome

+ 2 nonrenewable resources
+ 2 organs of the human digestive system
+ a food that provides carbohydrates
+ 2 ways the body defends against disease
+ 2 human body bones above the waist

# STRANGE BEHAVIORS

Ask students to name each animal behavior described below. Then they must try to think of another example of that same behavior. (Allow about 30 seconds per item.) What's the behavior?

+ A cat's fur grows thicker in cold weather. (adaptation)
+ A male peacock struts and bows in front of the female. (courtship or mating behavior)
+ A fish lies on the ocean floor and turns the color of the sand. (camouflage)
+ A skunk sprays a terrible-smelling liquid on a predator. (defensive behavior)
+ A lizard's tail breaks off when a predator grabs it, but grows back later. (regeneration)
+ A spider spins a web without being taught how to do it. (instinct)
+ A viceroy butterfly fools its prey by looking just like the poisonous monarch. (mimicry)
+ A fawn's coat has white spots. (protective coloration)
+ A goose hisses at any animal that comes into its area. (territoriality)

# WHAT'S THE MATTER?

Search the classroom for examples of objects or substances that show these different properties of matter. See how many students can find in five minutes. (Students may need to do a quick review of the meaning of some terms: solid, liquid, gas, fluid, solution, mixture, suspension, mass, density, organic)

- ✦ a solid
- ✦ a liquid
- ✦ a gas
- ✦ a fluid
- ✦ is magnetic
- ✦ a compound
- ✦ a mixture
- ✦ a solution
- ✦ a suspension

- ✦ has a mass greater than your own
- ✦ has a mass less than your own
- ✦ has a mass about the same as your math book

- ✦ a substance whose chemical make-up you know
- ✦ is less dense than water
- ✦ is more dense than water
- ✦ is made of a single element
- ✦ can scratch glass
- ✦ is an organic substance

# PICTURE THE CHANGE

Get ready to actually show changes in matter by drawing pictures of changes. Divide students into four groups. Give each group a large piece of drawing or mural paper. Ask them to bring pens, pencils, or markers, and be ready for drawing. Give two groups the task of drawing as many examples of physical changes in matter as they can draw in five minutes. Ask the other group to draw examples of chemical changes in matter.

| Examples of physical changes: | Examples of chemical changes: |
|---|---|
| breaking glass | baking a cake |
| separating rocks from sand | bleaching your hair |
| evaporating water | burning a candle |
| freezing popsicles | striking a match |
| rain condensing from clouds | frying an egg |
| clothes drying in a dryer | garbage rotting |
| blowing the top off a dandelion | a bicycle rusting |
| mixing up a milkshake | an old log decomposing |
| slicing bread | plants making oxygen |
| making chocolate milk | toast getting crisp and brown |
| whipping cream | food digesting |
| making lemonade | bread molding |

# SHOW SOME FORCE!

Get ready for some impromptu demonstrations of a good kind. Randomly call on 2 students at a time. Secretly give each pair one of the following words or phrases that name a force, motion, or concept related to force, energy, or motion. Ask the group to demonstrate that concept to the class. See if the class can tell what's being shown. Students may use any objects, movements, or people needed to demonstrate the concept. Do as many of the demonstrations as can fit into the short time space.

Concepts to demonstrate:

| | | |
|---|---|---|
| **gravity** | **acceleration** | **deceleration** |
| **centrifugal force** | **friction** | **air resistance** |
| **velocity** | **potential energy** | **inertia** |
| **momentum** | **kinetic energy** | **action-reaction** |

# WHAT'S THE QUESTION?

The list below gives answers to questions in physical science. But what are the questions? Tell students they will be given an answer to a question. They have 20 seconds to think of a question that would have that answer. (Students may think of more than one question. That's even better! Take as many questions as they can devise in the time allowed.)

And the answer is . . .

- ✦ **subatomic particles**
- ✦ **condensation**
- ✦ **viscosity**
- ✦ **a suspension**
- ✦ **an insulator**
- ✦ **static electricity**
- ✦ **buoyant force**
- ✦ **amplitude**
- ✦ **a watt**

- ✦ **an inorganic compound**
- ✦ **a machine consisting of only one part**
- ✦ **alternating current**
- ✦ **between 20 and 20,000 hertzes**
- ✦ **1 carbon atom and 2 oxygen atoms**
- ✦ **a supersaturated solution**
- ✦ **the blue litmus paper turns red**
- ✦ **radiation**
- ✦ **the magnet ends push away from each other**

# BONUS

Self-Awareness

*Self-Awareness*

Self-Awareness

**Self-Awareness**

Self-Awareness

*Self-Awareness*

Self-Awareness

**Self-Awareness**

Activities

# TOP 10 CHANGES

Everybody has times when they wish something was different. Ask students to think about what things or conditions they think should or could be changed. Tell them to write a list of at least ten things they want to change. When they are finished, they should go back and number the items in order of importance (with #1 being the most important.) Find time on another day for students to share their lists if they choose.

Example:

| | | | |
|---|---|---|---|
| 10 | today's weather | 5 | the homework policy |
| 9 | school hours | 4 | amount of gossiping in this class |
| 8 | the cost of movies | 3 | damage to the environment |
| 7 | my sister's boyfriend | 2 | war and hatred in the world |
| 6 | the mayor | 1 | my dad's health |

# THE BIG FIVE

It is a healthy exercise for all of us to think about ourselves and how we became the persons we are today. Ask students to consider what might be the major forces in shaping them as persons. Ask them to name the five most influential events, people, places, situations, or any other influences that have shaped their lives, their personalities, their abilities, their dreams, or their fears. They can write these down as their "big five." If there is time, students might write a short sentence about one. Find a time later when students who wish can share their lists. It is important for you to do this along with your students.

Example:

1. my place of birth and early years growing up in a remote rural area
2. my brother's birth defect
3. my grandmother
4. piano lessons that I've taken for 8 years
5. family's move to a big city when I was 9

# VALUE JUDGMENTS

Lead the class in a discussion of one of the following value questions:

- ✦ **Can you ever be too nice to someone?**
- ✦ **Are there ever times when you shouldn't tell the truth?**
- ✦ **Is it always best to keep a secret?**
- ✦ **When would it be okay to break a promise?**
- ✦ **When would it be okay to disobey an adult?**

# NOT RIGHT NOW!

Everyone has situations or events that they would like to avoid or postpone. That is why so many people are procrastinators.

Ask each student to tell something that he or she would rather not do "right" now.

Some examples might be:

- ✦ **face parents with a poor report card**
- ✦ **complete a spelling assignment**
- ✦ **take a test**
- ✦ **wash dishes**
- ✦ **start a diet**

# FINISH IT

Ask the students to respond to one of the following open-ended statements, and watch them discover their own feelings.

✦ **I feel happiest when . . .**
✦ **I'm a good friend because . . .**
✦ **The best thing that ever happened to me was . . .**
✦ **Nothing makes me angrier than . . .**
✦ **I'm really afraid of . . .**
✦ **Someday I want to . . .**
✦ **I can't stand people who . . .**

# SHOW YOU CARE

Many times young adults want to show others that they care about them, but they don't know the appropriate thing to do in some circumstances.

Ask your students to discuss what might be done to show how much they care in the following situations:

✦ **A friend is very unhappy over his or her parents' divorce or remarriage.**
✦ **Your best friend's pet died.**
✦ **Someone you love has a serious illness.**
✦ **Someone just did something embarrassing in front of other people.**
✦ **Your classmate's sister was killed in an automobile accident.**

# I'M IN CHARGE!

Young adults often feel that they never get to be in charge of anything; someone else is always in charge of them. Let them discuss what they would do if they were in charge of . . .

- ✦ **the school (Ask for serious responses.)**
- ✦ **their families (Would they change their family rules, etc.?)**
- ✦ **their town or city**
- ✦ **our country (What laws would they create or abolish?)**
- ✦ **the entire world (What could they do to promote peace?)**

# UNDER PRESSURE

Students of all ages experience peer pressure. Help students learn to deal with such situations by doing some role-playing in the classroom.

Select two students. One student will put pressure on the other one to do something that isn't quite right. The other student will try to resist the pressure without ruining the friendship. The "pressuring" friend might say:

- ✦ **Could I copy your homework? I forgot mine.**
- ✦ **Let's try this cigarette that I found in the bathroom.**
- ✦ **While I distract the clerk, you grab a couple of candy bars.**
- ✦ **Let's take that five-dollar bill that your mom left on the table.**
- ✦ **How about skipping school with me today? No one will know.**

# GOOD DEEDS

There is a saying that the best things in life are free.

Ask students to name some of the nice things that they can do for others without spending money. If there is time, make a list of the good deeds they name and post it as a reminder to everyone.

Some free good deeds:

- ✦ **Compliment a person on something he or she has done.**
- ✦ **Share something of yours with someone else.**
- ✦ **Listen to a friend's trouble.**
- ✦ **Offer to help with a problem or chore.**
- ✦ **Spend time with someone who is lonely.**
- ✦ **Introduce two of your friends to each other.**

---

# THE GOOD AND THE BAD

Most students grumble and complain about school. This activity stimulates them to think about what they like about school as well as what they dislike.

Make two lists on the board under the headings "good" and "bad." Let the students take turns. If the first student names something to go under the "bad" list, then the next student must name something to be placed in the "good" list.

**Some possible good things: place to see my old friends and meet new ones, it would be boring to be home all of the time, learn new things, etc.**

**Some possible bad things: too much work, can't talk enough, don't like the lunches, would rather be outside or watching TV, etc.**

# CHANGING ME

Ask each student to name something about him- or herself that has changed:

- ✦ **in the past twenty-four hours (clothing, hair style, mood)**
- ✦ **in the past seven days (age, weight, something learned to do)**
- ✦ **in the past year (joined Scouts, changed grades, broke leg)**
- ✦ **since birth (almost anything will fit here)**

Ask students to predict what changes they will experience in the next year, five years, or ten years.

# MY DREAM ROOM

Ask students to describe their dream classrooms by responding to these questions:

- ✦ **What color would the walls in your dream classroom be?**
- ✦ **What kind of furniture would be in it?**
- ✦ **How would the furniture be arranged?**
- ✦ **Would there be anything unusual about this room?**
- ✦ **Would your dream classroom have windows?**
- ✦ **What kind of desk would the teacher have?**
- ✦ **How would your dream classroom differ from your present classroom?**

# ONE TO TEN

Have students mentally rate themselves on a scale of 1 to 10 in relationship to these qualities or situations (1 is a poor rating and 10 is a high rating):

- ✦ I am a loyal friend.
- ✦ I am good at taking tests.
- ✦ I get along with other people.
- ✦ I can entertain myself.
- ✦ I am an athlete.
- ✦ I am cheerful.
- ✦ I practice good health habits.
- ✦ I control my temper.
- ✦ I am a positive influence on my peers.

# A FRIEND IS . . .

Ask students: "Who knows what a friend is?"

Probably all of the students will raise their hands. Call on students one at a time to complete this sentence: "A friend is someone who . . . ."

If there is time, post a long piece of craft paper on the bulletin board and let each student write and illustrate his or her version of "A friend is . . . ."

# NAME GAME

Have one student come to the front of the room and write his or her name in large letters vertically down one side of the chalkboard.

Then let the rest of the class write a name poem for that student by writing a descriptive word that begins with each letter of the name. Emphasize personal qualities rather than physical appearance.

Examples:

| | | |
|---|---|---|
| **Merry** | **Jolly** | **Lovely** |
| **Artistic** | **Outgoing** | **Eager** |
| **Restful** | **Enthusiastic** | **Sensitive** |
| **Talented** | | **Lively** |
| **Aware** | | **Intelligent** |
| | | **Even-tempered** |

# EXPRESS IT

Ask students to use sounds and body language to express how they would feel if in one of these situations:

✦ **Tomorrow is the day of the big field trip at school, and you just broke out in measles today.**

✦ **Your birthday present is exactly what you asked for!**

✦ **You are almost asleep, and you hear a strange noise in your closet.**

✦ **You lose sight of your parents at the airport fifteen minutes before your plane is scheduled to take off.**

✦ **You are trying to watch a concert, and everyone in front of you is taller than you are.**

✦ **You are last in the lunch line, and the cafeteria has run out of brownies.**

# MIRROR, MIRROR

Young adults need an opportunity to look closely at themselves. Give each student or pair of students a small hand mirror and these instructions:

✦ **Look closely at yourself in the mirror.**

✦ **While you look, describe yourself to a friend. What color are your eyes? What shape are your eyes? What shape is your mouth? Are your ears attached to your head all the way down or does your earlobe hang free at the end? Do you have freckles? Is your skin dark or light? Follow the shape of your hairline in the front. Does it look the same all the way across, or does it peak in the front?**

✦ **Place the mirror so that you can see only half of your face at a time. Do both halves look the same? If not, what is different about the halves?**

# A BETTER ME

Discuss the idea of self-improvement with your class. Point out that no one is perfect; there is something about each one of us that could be improved.

Give each student the opportunity to name something about him- or herself that could be improved. Remind the class that each person needs to be able to do this activity without anyone else making the participant feel uncomfortable or embarrassed.

If you will first name something about yourself that you want to improve, it will then be easier for students to evaluate themselves.

# INDEPENDENCE DAY

By the time students are in the intermediate grades, they may have daydreamed about living on their own. They usually think only of the freedom that they would have. They very seldom consider the cost and effort of providing for themselves.

As a class activity, have the students try to list all the goods and services they would have to pay for if they were living on their own.

They will name the obvious items (rent, groceries, telephone service). Try to guide them into discussion of the seemingly little items, like toothpaste and garbage collection fee, that they may skip.

# TO KNOW ME . . .

Let each student quickly draw a picture of him- or herself. Then ask them to pass the papers around the room for a minute or so to make sure that no one has his or her own drawing.

Let each student try to match up the drawing he or she has with the correct artist.

If there is time, post the pictures and number them. Let everyone make a list of the numbers and write the name of the correct student next to each one. Go over the list so that students can find out how many pictures they guessed correctly.

# MOVE TO THIS SIDE

Find out how your students are alike and different. Have all of the students stand on one side of the room. Then say, "Move to this side if . . . ." Finish your statement with one of the choices listed below. Students move from side to side to indicate their preferences.

"Move to this side (indicate side) if you'd rather . . ."

   . . . **wear yellow than blue.**

   . . . **eat liver than spinach.**

   . . . **do reading homework than math homework.**

   . . . **play soccer than watch TV.**

   . . . **eat pizza than hamburgers.**

   . . . **be spanked than grounded.**

---

# IT'S ME

Ask each student to write a brief description of him- or herself. Have them pass the papers to you. Read aloud each description and see if the rest of the class can identify the student. (Be sure to include a description of yourself!)

This activity can be extended by assigning each paper a number. Post the descriptions on a bulletin board. Let each student number a paper to match the numbers on the descriptions. Then, throughout the day or over a period of several days, students can list the students' names next to the numbers they think match the descriptions. Identify the correct names to let each student see how many he or she guessed correctly.

# INDEX